From Eve's Rib

From Eve's Rib

by

Gioconda Belli

translated by Steven F. White

CURBSTONE PRESS

The translator would like to express his gratitude to Charles Castaldi for his help on "Nicaragua Water Fire" and "The Dream Bearers." Special thanks are due to Greg Simon.

Some of these poems were first published in *Calyx* and *Arete*. We wish to thank them for permission to reprint them in this collection.

This publication was supported in part by donations, and by grants from The National Endowment for the Arts and The Connecticut Commission on The Arts, a state arts agency whose funds are recommended by the Governor and appropriated by the State Legislature.

ISBN: 0-915306-85-9
LC Number: 89-62124

Distributed in the U.S. by
The Talman Company
150 Fifth Avenue
New York, NY 10011

CURBSTONE PRESS
321 Jackson Street, Willimantic, CT 06226

contents

Introduction

Gioconda Belli, Nicaraguan and active inhabitant of her country's recent history, began to participate in the Sandinista struggle even as she first explored her identity as a woman. More than in the work of other women whose poetry has become accessible as their country demands attention in its ongoing struggle to be free, this dual identification is the leitmotif of all Gioconda's work.

As is true of a number of the Sandinista leaders, Gioconda was born into a family of the socially elite. Commitment to the rigors of the unequal battle against Somoza in her case also meant class betrayal on a more intimate level. And, as in so many Nicaraguan families, it has meant affections split by opposing allegiances: the conscious choice of life over death.

And so, Gioconda's poetic images frequently deal with sexuality and class, within the context of a nation's battle against generations of oppression. In the urban underground of the mid and late seventies, Belli worked with the Sandinista propaganda units; after the victory in 1979 she continued to use her advertising skills, but then within an exciting — if sometimes equally dangerous — context of vastly expanded possibility. A victorious and popular political leadership would supervise the establishment of a new society, drawing on deep cultural traditions and commited to addressing real human need.

The U.S.-backed efforts to destroy the fledgling revolution had not yet reached their later organizational heights. First priority tasks included educating an impoverished nation, attending to its most pressing health needs, substituting an ideology of dependancy with one of creative independence.

From the beginning, Gioconda lent her considerable talents to the ideological front. She was among those who discussed and helped to implement the first mass blows to individualism, racism, sexism, and a consumer's rather than a producer's mentality — in a people shell-shocked by death and intoxicated with a hard-won freedom. She worked with the written, audio and visual press, attended to the needs of foreign journalists, designed campaigns for everything from the prevention of maleria to the candidacies of Sandinistas running for electoral office.

And all the while she continued to be intensely conscious of herself as a woman, as mother of two daughters and a son — and as poet. Her first published book of verse had emerged at a moment of particular cultural intensity and within a group of socially conscious writers and artists; this was *Sobre la grama* (*On the Grass*), 1974.

Línea de fuego (*Line of Fire*) was also prior to the Sandinista victory and played a role in bringing worldwide attention to that struggle. The book appeared in 1978 after it had won the prestigious Casa de las Américas literary contest in Havana, Cuba.

Truenos y arco iris (*Thunder and Rainbow*) was one of the first titles from the ambitious publishing program launched immediately after the victory by Editorial Nueva Nicaragua; it made its appearance in 1982. Then there was *Amor insurrecto* (*Insurrectional Love*) in 1985, and the volume from which this collection takes its title — *De la costilla de Eve* (*From Eve's Rib*) — in 1987.[*]

The following year, 1988, Gioconda published her first novel, a story of love, war, and indigenous roots called *La mujer habitada* (*The Inhabited Woman*). But it is her poetry that most concerns us here.

Over and over, there is a strong parallel in these poems. The urgency of love between partners becomes a metaphor for the will of a people to be free. The intensity of conquest in sexual fulfillment becomes the insatiable need of a nation to control its destiny, and vice versa. Man and woman, satiating one another (Gioconda's images are exclusively heterosexual) move beyond the intimacy of the couple and evoke as well the powerful struggle of the Nicaraguan people.

---

[*]The Spanish and English books are not identical in content.

Gioconda's is a poetic that draws on the deep drama of human emotions caught as well as freed by revolutionary war. Her style often utilizes the skillful publicist's knowledge that the repetition of one simple word or phrase is sometimes more effective than the unusual but sometimes convoluted image. The simple profundity of her verse has provoked several of Nicaragua's most popular singers to set some of her poems to music, and she has had the joy of hearing her poems sung enthusiastically in a public square by tens of thousands of voices.

Gioconda Belli's is a poetry alive with the landscape of her country: its wildness and beauty as well as its heroic struggle. This first — and to date, only — bilingual publication in the United States allows us to enter the rich world of this important contemporary poet. We can listen to the woman who urges: "...The dream bearers knew their power/and therefore were not surprised/And they also knew that life had engendered them/to protect itself from the death announced in the prophecies./And so they defended their lives even with death./And so they cultivated gardens of dreams...."

Margaret Randall
Albuquerque, New Mexico/Spring 1989

FROM EVE'S RIB

Y Dios me hizo mujer

Y Dios me hizo mujer,
de pelo largo,
ojos,
nariz y boca de mujer.
Con curvas
y pliegues
y suaves hondonadas
y me cavó por dentro,
me hizo un taller de seres humanos.
Tejió delicadamente mis nervios
y balanceó con cuidado
el número de mis hormonas.
Compuso mi sangre
y me inyectó con ella
para que irrigara
todo mi cuerpo;
nacieron así las ideas,
los sueños,
el instinto.
Todo lo que creó suavemente
a martillazos de soplidos
y taladrazos de amor,
las mil y una cosas que me hacen mujer todos los días
por las que me levanto orgullosa
todas las mañanas
y bendigo mi sexo.

And God Made Me Woman

And God made me woman,
with the long hair,
the eyes,
the nose and the mouth of a woman.
With curves
and folds
and soft hollows . . .
God dug into me,
made a workshop in me for human beings,
delicately wove my nerves,
and carefully balanced
the number of my hormones,
composed my blood
and injected me with it
so that it would irrigate
my entire body.
And so ideas were born,
dreams,
instinct,
everything God gently created
with hammering whispers
and the drilling motion of love,
the thousand and one things that make me woman every day,
that make me proud every morning
when I arise
and bless my sex.

Dime

Dime que no me conformarás nunca,
ni me darás la felicidad de la resignación,
sino la felicidad que duele de los elegidos,
los que pueden abarcar el mar y el cielo con sus ojos
y llevar el Universo dentro de sus cuerpos:

Y yo te vestiré con lodo y te daré a comer tierra
para que conozcas el sabor de vientre del mundo.

Escribiré sobre tu cuerpo la letra de mis poemas
para que sientas en tí el dolor del alumbramiento.

Te vendrás conmigo: Haremos un rito del amor
y una explosión de cada uno de nuestros actos.

No habrá paredes que nos acorralen,
ni techo sobre nuestras cabezas.

Olvidaremos la palabra
y tendremos nuestra propia manera de entendernos;
ni los días, ni las horas podrán atraparnos
porque estaremos escondidos del tiempo en la niebla.

Crecerán las ciudades,
se extenderá la humanidad invadiéndolo todo;
nosotros dos seremos eternos,
porque siempre habrá un lugar del mundo que nos cubra
y un pedazo de tierra que nos alimente.

Tell Me

Tell me that you will never allow me to conform,
that you will impart not a subdued happiness,
but the painful kind of the chosen few,
who embrace sea and sky with their eyes
and bear the Universe within their bodies:

And I will dress you in clay and have you eat earth,
so you can savor the womb of this world.

I will write the words of my poems on your body,
so you can sense the internal pain of birth.

Come with me! We'll make a ritual of our love,
an explosion of each and every movement.

There will be no walls enclosing us,
or any roof above our heads.

We will forget the word
in our own new way of understanding each other;
we will escape the snare of days and hours,
hidden from time in the fog.

Cities will grow;
humanity's total invasion will spread.
But the two of us will be eternal,
For in the world we will always find shelter somewhere
and a piece of land to nourish us.

Menstruación

Tengo
la "enfermedad"
de las mujeres.

Mis hormonas
están alborotadas,
me siento parte
de la naturaleza.

Todos los meses
esta comunión
del alma
y el cuerpo;
este sentirse objeto
de leyes naturales
fuera de control;
el cerebro recogido
volviéndose vientre.

Menstruation

I've got
"the curse"
of women.

My hormones
are in turmoil.
I feel one
with nature.

Each month
this joining
of body
and soul.
Feeling subject
to uncontrollable
laws of nature,
my brain cramps,
becoming a womb.

Maternidad

Mi cuerpo,
como tierra agradecida,
se va extendiendo.

Ya las planicies de mi vientre
van cogiendo la forma
de una redonda colina palpitante,
mientras por dentro,
en quién sabe qué misterio
de agua, sangre y silencio
va creciendo como un puño que se abre
el hijo que sembraste
en el centro de mi fertilidad.

Maternity

My body,
like fertile earth,
is expanding.

Already the plains of my womb
are becoming
a round, beating hill,
and within,
in a mystery
of water, blood and silence
the child you sowed
opens like a fist
in the center of my fertility.

Parto

Me acuerdo
cuando nació mi hija.

Yo era un solo dolor miedoso,
esperando ver salir de entre mis piernas
un sueño de nueve meses
con cara y sexo.

Birth

I remember
my daughter's birth.

I was fear and pain
waiting to see between my legs
an emerging nine-month-old dream
with a face and a sex.

¿Qué sos Nicaragua?

¿Qué sos
sino un triangulito de tierra
perdido en la mitad del mundo?

¿Qué sos
sino un vuelo de pájaros

> guardabarrancos
> cenzontles
> colibríes?

¿Qué sos
sino un ruido de ríos
llevándose las piedras pulidas y brillantes
dejando pisadas de agua por los montes?

¿Qué sos
sino pechos de mujer hechos de tierra,
lisos, puntudos y amenazantes?

¿Qué sos
sino cantar de hojas en árboles gigantes.
verdes, enmarañados y llenos de palomas?

¿Qué sos
sino dolor y polvo y gritos en la tarde,
— "gritos de mujeres, como de parto" — ?

¿Qué sos
sino puño crispado y bala en boca?

¿Qué sos, Nicaragua,
para dolerme tanto?

What Are You Nicaragua?

What are you —
a little triangle of earth
lost in the middle of the world?

What are you —
a flight of birds
> *guardabarrancos*
> *cenzontles*
> hummingbirds?

What are you —
a roar of rivers
bearing polished, shiny stones
leaving footprints of water in the mountains?

What are you —
a woman's breasts made of earth,
smooth, pointed and threatening?

What are you —
singing of leaves in gigantic trees,
green, tangled and filled with doves?

What are you —
pain and dust and screams in the afternoon,
"screams like those of women in labor"?

What are you —
clenched fist and loaded gun?

What are you Nicaragua
to hurt me so?

Metamorfosis

La enredadera
se me está saliendo
por las orejas.

Mis ojos se han convertido
en pistilos movibles
y mi boca está repleta
de flores moradas.

Mientras camino
sigo llenando de hojas
la casa.

Mis ramas estorban en el cuarto,
sigo enredándome en todo;
ya mi nariz
también se ha puesto verde
y mis olores han cambiado,
tropiezo con los muebles
y mis piernas están rompiendo
los ladrillos,
buscando la tierra,
enredándome.

Mi pelo ya no me deja moverme,
está abrazado a las paredes,
los brazos se han hundido
sólo me quedan los dedos
mientras mi cuerpo
se ha vuelto tronco.

Con mis dedos
me toco toda

Metamorphosis

The vines
are twisting
from my ears.

My eyes have become
pistils in motion
and purple flowers
flow from my mouth.

As I walk,
the house fills
with my leaves.

My branches block the room,
and I'm tangled up in everything.
My nose has already turned green, too,
and I no longer smell the same.
I bump into the furniture,
and my legs are breaking through bricks
in search of land,
tangling me up even more.

Now that my hair pushes against the walls,
I can barely move.
My arms have shrunk away,
leaving just my fingers,
while my body's
become a trunk.

With my fingers,
I touch my new

re-conociéndome
entre las hojas
y las ramitas
y las flores que llenan mi boca
y han teñido mis dientes.

Me repasan mis dedos
y su contacto es abono
para mis ramas que crecen
y ya por fin,
después de mucho resistir,
se han rendido las manos
y están saliendo pullitas
de las uñas.

Mi boca llena de flores moraditas
ha cuajado mi cuerpo
y estoy enredadera,
metamorfoseada,
espinosa,
sola,
hecha naturaleza.

self all over
among the leaves
and twigs
and flowers that fill my mouth
and stain my teeth.

My fingers explore me
with a touch fertile
for my growing branches,
and finally,
after so much resistance,
my hands give in
and tiny thorns sprout
from my nails.

The purple flowers from my mouth
cover my body,
and in my metamorphosis
I am a twisting mass of vines,
thorny,
alone,
one with nature.

Vestidos de dinamita

Me tengo que ir a comprar las pinturas con las que me disfrazo todos los días para que nadie adivine que tengo los ojos chiquitos — como de ratón o de elefante —. Estoy yéndome desde hace una hora pero me retiene el calor de mi cuarto y la soledad que, por esta vez, me está gustando y los libros que tengo desparramados en mi cama como hombres con los que me voy acostando, en una orgía de piernas y de brazos que me levantan el desgano de vivir y me arañan los pezones, el sexo, y me llenan de un semen especial hecho de letras que me fecundan y no quiero salir a la calle con la cara seria cuando quisiera reír a carcajadas sin ningún motivo en especial más que este sentirme preñada de palabras, en lucha contra la sociedad de consumo que me llama con sus escaparates llenos de cosas inalcanzables y a las que rechazo con todas mis hormonas femeninas cuando recuerdo las caras gastadas y tristes de las gentes en mi pueblo que deben haber amanecido hoy como amanecen siempre y como seguirán amaneciendo hasta que no nos vistamos de dinamita y nos vayamos a invadir palacios de gobierno, ministerios, cuarteles. . . con un fosforito en la mano.

Dressed in Dynamite

I have to go buy the makeup I use to disguise myself each day so that no one finds out my eyes are tiny — like a mouse's or an elephant's. I've wanted to leave for an hour, but the warmth of my room keeps me from going. So does the solitude that, at least for now, I'm enjoying. And the books spread out on my bed are like men I've made love with in an orgy of legs and arms that awaken my passion for life, biting my nipples, my sex, and filling me with a special semen made from letters fecundating me, and I don't want to go outside with such a serious face when I'd rather be laughing out loud for no other reason except this feeling of being word-pregnant, struggling against a consumer society that entices me with its store windows filled with unattainable things, things I reject with all my feminine hormones when I remember the spent and sad faces of my people who woke up today the way they always wake up and will continue waking up until we dress ourselves in dynamite and invade government centers, ministries, headquarters. . .with a match in our hands.

Yo, la que te quiere

Yo soy tu indómita gacela,
el trueno que rompe la luz sobre tu pecho.
Yo soy el viento desatado en la montaña
y el fulgor concentrado del fuego del ocote.
Yo caliento tus noches,
encendiendo volcanes en mis manos,
mojándote los ojos con el humo de mis cráteres.
Yo he llegado hasta vos vestida de lluvia y de recuerdo,
riendo la risa inmutable de los años.
Yo soy el inexplorado camino,
la claridad que rompe la tiniebla.
Yo pongo estrellas entre tu piel y la mía
y te recorro entero,
sendero tras sendero,
descalzando mi amor,
desnudando mi miedo.
Yo soy un nombre que canta y te enamora
desde el otro lado de la luna,
soy la prolongación de tu sonrisa y tu cuerpo.
Yo soy algo que crece,
algo que ríe y llora.
Yo,
la que te quiere.

I Am the Woman Who Loves You

I am your untamed gazelle,
thunder shattering light on your chest.
I am the wind unleashed in the mountain
and the intense radiance of the *ocote* tree's fire.
I warm your nights,
lighting volcanoes in my hands,
making you cry with the smoke from my craters.
I come to you wrapped in rain and memories,
laughing the unchanging laughter of the years.
I am the unexplored road,
brightness shattering darkness.
With stars, I join your skin and mine
and I wander your entire being
trail after trail,
unlacing my love,
undressing my fear.
I am a name that sings and entices you
from the dark side of the moon,
I am the extension of your smile and your body.
I am something that grows,
something that laughs and cries.
I am the woman
who loves you.

Recorriéndote

Quiero morder tu carne,
salada y fuerte,
empezar por tus brazos hermosos
como ramas de ceibo,
seguir por ese pecho con el que sueñan
        mis sueños
ese pecho-cueva donde se esconde mi cabeza
hurgando la ternura,
ese pecho que suena a tambores y vida continuada.
Quedarme allí un rato largo
enredando mis manos
en ese bosquecito de arbustos que te crece
suave y negro bajo mi piel desnuda,
seguir después hacia tu ombligo
hacia ese centro donde te empieza el cosquilleo,
irte besando, mordiendo,
hasta llegar allí
a ese lugarcito
— apretado y secreto —
que se alegra ante mi presencia
que se adelanta a recibirme
y viene a mí
en toda su dureza de macho enardecido.
Bajar luego a tus piernas
firmes como tus convicciones guerrilleras,
esas piernas donde tu estatura se asienta,
con las que vienes a mí,
con las que me sostienes,
las que enredas en la noche entre las mías
blandas y femeninas.
Besar tus pies, amor,
que tanto tienen aún que recorrer sin mí
y volver a escalarte

Exploring You

I want to taste
your salty, strong flesh,
start with your arms as splendid
as the branches of a ceiba tree,
then your chest like a cave
in a dream I've dreamt,
chest-cave where my head lies hidden,
searching for tenderness,
that chest sounding like drums
and life's never-ending flow.
I want to stay there a long time,
letting my fingers tangle
the black and gentle forest
growing beneath my naked skin,
and move then to your navel,
to that center where you start to tremble,
kissing and biting you
until I reach
the close and secret realm
that welcomes me,
aroused, moving toward me
with a male's hardened fire.
Slide down to your legs
as strong as your guerrilla-convictions,
the legs that support your whole body,
and bring you to me,
the legs you use to hold me,
and wrap at night around mine,
so different, soft and feminine.
I would kiss your feet, my love —
they still have so many roads to travel without me,
and then I would go back

hasta apretar tu boca con la mía,
hasta llenarme toda de tu saliva
                              y tu aliento
hasta que entrés en mí
con la fuerza de la marea
y me invadás con tu ir y venir
de mar furioso
y quedemos los dos tendidos y sudados
en la arena de las sábanas.

to press my lips against yours,
to absorb your saliva, your breath
until you enter me
with the force of the tide
invading me with the ebb and flow
of a furious sea,
leaving us both sweaty and spent
on linen sands.

Al comandante Marcos

El ruido de la metralla nos dejó con la puerta en las narices.
La puerta de tu vida cerrada de repente
en la madera que te duerme y acurruca en el vientre de la tierra.

No puedo creer tu muerte,
tan sin despedida.
— sólo ese lejano presentimiento de aquella noche,
          ¿te acordás? —
en que lloré rabiosamente viéndote dormido,
sabiéndote pájaro migratorio
en rápida fuga de la vida.

Después,
cuando partiste,
cuando agarraste el peligro por las crines
y te sabía rodeado de furiosos perros,
empecé a creer que eras indestructible.
¿Cómo poder creer en el final de tus manos,
de tus ojos, de tu palabra?
¿Cómo creer en tu final cuando vos eras todo principio;
la chispa, el primer disparo, la orden de fuego,
los planes, la calma?

Pero allí estaba la noticia en el periódico
y tu foto mirándome sin verme
y esa definitiva sensación de tu ausencia
corriéndome por dentro sin consuelo,
dejando muy atrás la frontera de las lágrimas,
echándose en mis venas,
reventando contra todas mis esquinas.

To Comandante Marcos

The sound of machine gun fire slammed the door in our faces.
The door of your life suddenly shut
inside the wood that cuddles you to sleep in the earth's womb.

I can't believe your death,
so lacking in goodbyes —
only that distant premonition one night, do you remember?
I cried furiously seeing you asleep,
knowing that you were a migrating bird
flying swiftly through life.

Afterwards,
when you left,
when you grabbed danger by the mane
and I knew you surrounded by ravenous dogs,
I began to think you were indestructible.
How could I believe your hands would end,
your eyes, your word?
How could I believe you could end when you were always
                                        the beginning;
the spark, the first shot, the order to fire,
the plans, composure itself?

But there it was in the newspaper —
your photograph looking at me, not seeing me,
and the absolute feeling of your absence
rushing within me inconsolably,
leaving the border of tears far behind,
pouring into my veins,
crashing against every corner of my body.

Va pasando el tiempo
y va siendo más grande el hueco de tu nombre,
los minutos cargados de tu piel,
del canto rítmico de tu corazón,
de todo lo que ahora nada en mi cerebro
y te lleva y te trae como el flujo y reflujo
de una marea de sangre,
donde veo rojo de dolor y de rabia
y escribo sin poder escribir este llanto infinito,
redondo y circular como tu símbolo,
donde no puedo vislumbrar tu final
y siento solamente con la fuerza del abrazo,
de la lluvia,
de los caballos en fuga,
tu principio.

Time goes by
yet the emptied space of your name grows larger,
so do the loaded minutes of your skin,
of your heart's rhythmic song,
of everything that swims now in my brain
and takes you away and brings you closer
like the ebb and flow of a tide of blood,
where my eyes see red from pain and anger
and I write, unable to write, this infinite sobbing
like your round, circular symbol,
where I can't envisage your end.
What remains for me —
strong as an embrace,
as rain,
as fleeing horses —
is your beginning.

Patria libre: 19 de julio de 1979

Extraño sentir este sol otra vez
y ver el júbilo de las calles alborotadas de gente,
las banderas rojinegras por todas partes
y una nueva cara de la ciudad que despierta
con el humo de las llantas quemadas
y las altas hileras de barricadas.

El viento me va dando en plena cara
donde circulan libres polvo y lágrimas,
respiro hondo para convencerme de que no es un sueño,
que allá está el Motastepe, el Momotombo, el lago,
que lo hicimos al fin,
que lo logramos.
Tantos años creyendo esto contra viento y marea,
creyendo que este día era posible,
aun después de saber la muerte de Ricardo, de Pedro, de Carlos. . .
de tantos otros que nos arrancaron,
ojos que nos sacaron,
sin poder dejarnos nunca ciegos a este día
que nos revienta hoy entre las manos.

Cuántas muertes se me agolpan en la garganta,
queridos muertos con los que alguna vez soñamos este sueño
y recuerdo sus caras, sus ojos,
la seguridad con que conocieron esta victoria,
la generosidad con que la construyeron,
ciertos de que esta hora feliz aguardaba en el futuro
y que por ella bien valía la pena morir.

Me duele como parto esta alegría.
Me duele no poder despertarlos para que vengan a ver

Patria Libre: July 19, 1979

Strange to feel this sun again
and to see the jubilation of streets swarming with people,
the red and black flags everywhere
and a new face of the city awakening
to the smoke of burning tires
and the high lines of barricades.

The wind hits me full in the face
where dust and tears mix freely,
I take a deep breath to convince myself it is not a dream,
that in the distance I can see Motastepe and Momotombo, the lake,
that we did it, finally,
we really did it.
So many years believing this against wind and tide,
believing this day was possible,
even after the deaths of Ricardo, Pedro, and Carlos
and so many others they ripped from our side,
eyes they gouged out,
without ever blinding us to this day,
bursting now in our hands.

So many deaths knot my throat,
beloved dead with whom we once dreamed this dream,
and I remember their faces, their eyes,
their certainty in knowing this victory,
the generosity with which they built it,
so sure that this happy moment would arrive,
worthy of their deaths.

This happiness hurts like giving birth.
It hurts that they cannot wake to see

este pueblo gigante saliendo de la noche,
con la cara tan fresca y la sonrisa tan encima de los labios,
como que la hubieran estado acumulando
y la soltaran en tropeles, de repente.

Hay miles de sonrisas saliendo de los cajones,
de las casas quemadas, de los adoquines,
sonrisas vestidas de colores como pedazos de sandía,
de melón o níspero.

Yo siento que tengo que gozarme y regocijarme
como lo hubieran hecho mis hermanos dormidos,
gozarme con este triunfo tan de ellos,
tan hijo de su carne y de su sangre
y en medio del bullicio de este día tan azul,
montada en el camión,
pasando entre las calles, en medio de las caras hermosas
            de mi gente,
quisiera que me nacieran brazos para abrazarlos a todos
y decirles a todos que los quiero,
que la sangre nos ha hermanado con su vínculo doloroso,
que estamos juntos para aprender a hablar de nuevo,
a caminar de nuevo;
que en este futuro — herencia de muerte y de gemidos —
sonarán estrepitosas descargas de martillo,
rafagazos de torno,
zumbidos de machete;
que éstas serán las armas
para sacarle luz a las cenizas,
cemento, casas, pan, a las cenizas;
que no desmayaremos, nunca nos rendiremos,
que sabremos como ellos
pensar en los días hermosos que verán otros ojos
y en esta borrachera de libertad
que invade las calles, mece los árboles,

this massive people emerging from the night,
with radiant faces and smiles so present on their lips
as if they had been storing them
and then decided to release them all at once.

Thousands of smiles rising from the rubble,
burnt houses, paving stones,
smiles the color of sliced watermelons,
cantaloupes or medlars.

I feel I should rejoice
as my sleeping comrades would have done,
enjoy this triumph that so belongs to them,
such a child of their flesh and blood.
And amidst the tumult of this bright day,
standing on the back of the truck,
riding through the streets, surrounded by the resplendent faces
        of my people,
I wish I had enough arms to embrace each one,
to tell them all I love them,
for blood has joined us with its painful link,
and we are together in this learning to speak again,
to walk again.
In this future, this legacy of death and mourning,
loud volleys of hammer blows will echo,
lathes will spin and whirl,
and machetes will ring,
for these will be our weapons now
to draw light from the ashes,
cement, houses, bread from the ashes;
for we will never give up, we will never surrender.
Like our dead, we, too, will build
the beauty of days to come for other eyes to see,
and in this drunken spirit of freedom
spreading through the streets, swaying trees,

sopla el humo de los incendios
que nos acompañen
        tranquilos
           felices
               siempre-vivos
                  nuestros muertos.

blowing smoke from fires
let our dead be with us —
                fulfilled
                        happy
                                always living.

La sangre de otros

Leo los poemas de los muertos
yo que estoy viva
yo que viví para reírme y llorar
y gritar Patria Libre o Morir
sobre un camión
el día que llegamos a Managua.

Leo los poemas de los muertos,
veo las hormigas sobre la grama,
mis pies descalzos,
tu pelo lacio,
espalda encorvada sobre la reunión.

Leo los poemas de los muertos
y siento que esta sangre con que nos amamos,
no nos pertenece.

The Blood of Others

I read the poems of the dead.
I survived.
I lived to laugh and cry
and I shouted *Patria Libre o Morir*
from the back of a truck
the day we reached Managua.

I read the poems of the dead,
watching the ants on the grass,
my bare feet,
your straight hair,
your back arched at the meeting.

I read the poems of the dead.
Does the blood in our bodies that lets us love each other
belong to us?

Soñar para despertar soñando

¿Quién es esa que corre en los cielos
con su flotante bufanda de estrellas,
con nuestra tierra y el sol rondando
como abejas su corazón en flor?
Sus pies van en los vientos
donde el espacio es hondo.
Sus ojos son velados, nebulosos,
vuela en la noche en busca
de un amante lejano.

— *James Oppenheim*

Ya que no me queda más que soñar
y el tiempo de esperar parece una playa que nunca se termina,
levantaré las noches, los umbrales de la madrugada
y me lanzaré al sueño
como una flotante bailarina sin velos,
desnuda para que nada me estorbe,
para que el cielo me vea como soy
y puedan decidir las estrellas
qué planeta me asignarán de residencia,
en qué revolución me sembrarán

— porque también debe haber en las galaxias;
todo está en constante movimiento.

Me harán fertilizar con todo el llanto
evaporado desde mis ojos
y también con mi sudor, mis heces,
todo lo que segrego porque vivo y funciono
y lo que mi cuerpo hace o destruye,
tiene razón de ser y es hermoso.

To Dream in Order to Wake up Dreaming

Who is the runner in the skies —
With her blowing scarf of stars,
And our earth and sun hovering like bees
            about her blossoming heart!
Her feet are on the winds where space is deep;
Her eyes are nebulous and veiled;
She hurries through the night to a far lover.
                                    — James Oppenheim

Since now there is nothing for me to do but dream,
for the time of waiting is like a never-ending beach,
I'll lift the nights, the thresholds of dawn,
and hurl myself into the dream
like a dancer floating with no veils,
naked so nothing hinders me,
so the sky sees me as I am
and the stars can decide
what planet they'll give me as a place to stay,
in what revolution they'll let me grow —

        because there must be revolutions in the galaxies;
        all things are forever moving.

Stars will make me fertile,
using my dried tears,
my sweat and feces, too,
everything my body secretes, because I live and function
and whatever my body produces or destroys
has a reason for being and is beautiful.

Allí, en ese vacío del espacio
— quieto, perturbador, amenazante —
como éste en el que ahora estoy,
habré de encontrarlo, de verlo, de tocarlo.
Desde el asteroide B-612, lo veré conformarse como una nebulosa;
piernas, manos, acento, labios,
ojos para verme como nadie me ha visto
— hasta el fondo, sin miedo, ni prejuicios —.
Sentiré que me cerca, me acuna,
que recoge mis poemas y los lee y le gustan,
que traspasamos juntos lluvias de meteoritos
y calla o es misterio
o transparente, me deja contemplarlo,
ver cómo corre su sangre,
trabaja su cerebro,
me ama con el fuego prendido de los astros,
me toma de la mano
en paseos inmensos por las Siete Cabritas,
los anillos de Saturno, por las lunas de Júpiter,
y nos vamos saciando de la sed de universo.

Después,
lo sé,
empezaré a soñar otra vez con nuestra Luna,
con el planeta Tierra,
con un lugar muy definido
en el ombligo de un largo continente,
y empezaré a contarle del sol entre los árboles,
del calor, de las selvas,
el canto de los pájaros
y las hermosas voces de las gentes.
Le haré cantos con truenos,
le hablaré de las manos callosas,
de la guerra, del triunfo,
de lo que nos costó, lo que sufrimos,
lo que ahora gozamos, trabajamos, hacemos.

There, in that emptiness —
quiet, perturbing, threatening —
like the void I'm living now,
I'll find him, see him, touch him.
From asteroid B-612, I'll see him take shape like a nebula;
legs, hands, accent, lips,
eyes to see me like no one ever has —
deeply, with no fear, no biases.
I'll feel him enclose me, cuddle me,
gather my poems, read them and be pleased.
While we travel together through meteor showers,
he falls silent or is a mystery
or, becoming transparent, lets me contemplate
the way his blood flows,
the workings of his brain,
the way he loves me with the lit fire of stars,
taking my hand
on immense journeys by the Seven Sisters,
the rings of Saturn, Jupiter's moons,
both of us quenching our thirst for the universe.

Later,
I know,
I'll begin to dream again of our moon,
the planet Earth,
a very specific place
in the navel of a large continent,
and I'll begin to tell him about the sun through the trees,
the warmth, the jungles,
the songs of birds
and the beautiful voices of the people.
I'll make him chants from thunder,
speak to him of calloused hands,
the war, the triumph,
how much it cost us, how much we suffered.
What we now enjoy, we work at, we do.

Sentiré la punzante nostalgia de la tierra mojada,
pensaré en las cosas que he dejado de hacer
por andar arrebujada en sueños, conociendo planetas,
y nos vendremos juntos
aprovechando la conjunción de los astros.

Me dirá que tenía razón
que es bello este lugar,
mis volcanes tendidos sobre el paisaje como una mujer
          de pechos desordenados,
los lagos, las banderas, las sonrisas
y me dirá:
Trabaja, mujer, trabaja,
trabajemos,
que el sueño está aquí mismo,
en este mismo sitio.

¿Para qué otros mundos
otras constelaciones?

Aquí mismo quedémonos despiertos
en medio de esta
recién nacida, amenazada,
estrella.

I'll feel the damp earth piercing my nostalgia
and consider everything I have missed,
abandoned to my dreams, journeying to other planets,
and so, together, we will return
benefiting from the conjunction of the stars.

He'll tell me I was right,
for this place is truly beautiful,
my volcanoes stretched out on the landscape like a woman
          of wild breasts,
the lakes, the flags and smiles
and he'll say to me:
work, woman, work,
let's work,
for the dream is right here
right here where we are.

Why go to other worlds
or other constellations?
Let's wake up, here,
in the center of this
new, endangered
star.

Ayúdame a creer que no seremos
los últimos pobladores de la tierra

Mi deseo de vos, amado,
es como el viento en las colinas de Waslala,
corriendo sin parar
y siempre regresando.

Jadeo de tristeza
y lloro de amor encerrada
como tigre enjaulado
en las noches,
oyendo tu palabra,
tu cabeza en la almohada cercana.

Qué seré para vos, amado,
en este trapiche
donde no quedará nada en pie de nuestra estatura,
en estos días en que todo es más vivo
porque cercana está la muerte
y yo te abrazo mientras apretadamente
nos cercan las manadas de lobos
e incierto es el brillo titilante de las estrellas,
aunque verdadero es el amor, los valores trascendentales
de la historia, la belleza
y esta fe en que todo podrá perecer
en la locura atómica de estos tiempos,
pero que ese aliento de vida que tuvimos
resurgirá en la constante movilidad de la materia,
aunque ya no estarán nuestros cuerpos
y estos cantos serán alimento del humo en la hecatombe.

Por eso, amado,
hoy más que nunca,

Help Me Believe We Will Not Be the Last People on Earth

My longing for you
is like the wind sweeping
across the hills of Waslala —
endlessly returning.

Sadness steals my breath,
and at night I cry this love, imprisoned
like a caged tiger,
listening to your words,
your head resting so close on the pillow.

What shall I be to you, my love, in these times
like a cane press, into which we are fed
and nothing is left standing,
in times like these when things are more alive
because of their nearness to death,
and I embrace you while
packs of wolves surround us, circling closer,
and the shimmering stars are no longer steadfast.
But we feel the truth of love, the transcendent values
of history, beauty
and this faith that even though all things might perish
in atomic madness,
the breath of life we had will come forth again
in matter's constant movement,
even if our bodies ceased to exist
and these songs fueled the holocaust's smoke.

That's why, my love,
today more than ever, I listen

oigo tictaquear el reloj,
el momento que se escurre entre los dedos
y estoy triste
ante la certeza del huracán.

Por eso me siento a blandir estos poemas,
a construir contra viento y marea
un pequeño espacio de felicidad,
a tener fe en que no podrá terminar todo esto
— el rostro de Saslaya
— el rojo de las flores

que no seremos los últimos pobladores de la tierra,
que se hundirá,
sin nosotros a cuestas,
el imperio.

to the ticking of the watch,
the minutes slipping through my fingers,
and the certainty of the hurricane
saddens me.

That's why I'm determined to wield these poems
and build a small place of happiness
come hell or high water,
and maintain the faith that all this cannot end
— Saslaya's face
— the flowers' red color

that we will not be the last people on earth,
that we'll be spared
when the Empire
destroys itself.

Canto de guerra

Vendrá la guerra, amor
y en el combate no habrá tregua
ni freno para el canto
sino poesía naciendo del hueco oscuro
del cañón de los fusiles.

Vendrá la guerra, amor
y nos confundiremos en las trincheras
cavando el futuro en las faldas de la Patria
deteniendo a punta de corazón y fuego
las hordas de bárbaros
pretendiendo llevarse lo que somos y amamos.

Vendrá la guerra, amor
y yo me envolveré en tu sombra invencible,
como fiera leona
protegeré la tierra de mis hijos
y nadie detendrá esta victoria
armada de futuro hasta los dientes.

Aunque ya no nos veamos
y hasta puedan morirse los recuerdos,
te lo juro por vos,
te lo juro apretando a Nicaragua
como niña de pecho:

¡No pasarán, amor
los venceremos!

Warsong

The war will come, my love,
and there will be no truce in combat,
no stopping of the song,
only poetry emerging in birth from the dark
emptied spaces of rifles.

The war will come, my love,
and we'll be mixed with others
digging the future in the soft slopes of our land,
using our hearts and fire
to hold back the hords of barbarians
who are trying to erase all that we are and love.

The war will come, my love,
and I'll wrap myself in your invincible shadow,
like a fierce lioness
I will protect my children's land
and no one will halt this victory
armed to the teeth with the future.

Even if we never see each other again,
even though memories may die,
I swear, because of you,
I swear, holding Nicaragua
like a child to my breast:

They will not pass, my love,
we will defeat them!

Permanencia

Duro decir:
Te amo,
mira cuánto tiempo, distancia y pretensión
he puesto ante el horror de esa palabra,
esa palabra como serpiente
que viene sin hacer ruido, ronda
y se niega una, dos, tres, cuatro, muchas veces,
ahuyentándola como un mal pensamiento,
una debilidad,
un desliz,
algo que no podemos permitirnos

      ese temblor primario
      que nos acerca al principio del mundo,
      al lenguaje elemental del roce o el
      contacto,
      la oscuridad de la caverna,
      el hombre y la mujer
      lamiéndose el espanto del estruendo —

Reconocer,
ante el espejo,
la huella,
la ausencia de cuerpos entrelazados hablándose.

Sentir que hay
un amor feroz
enjaulado a punta de razones,
condenado a morir de inanición,
sin darse a nadie más
obseso de un rostro inevitable.

Permanence

So hard to say:
I love you.
Look at all the time, distance and pretence
I've created out of my fear of those words,
those words like a serpent,
slithering in silence, threatening:
denied once, twice, so many times,
dismissed like an evil thought,
a weakness,
a mistake,
something we can't allow

      — a shudder so basic
      that it takes us to the beginning of the world,
      to the elemental language of touch,
      the cave's darkness,
      the man and the woman
      licking their fear of thunder from each other —

To look in the mirror
and recognize
the traces,
the absence of bodies embracing and talking to each other.

To sense
a fierce love
trapped in the cage of reason,
condemned to die of starvation,
without giving itself to anyone else,
obsessed with an inevitable face.

Pasar por días
de levantar la mano,
formar el gesto del reencuentro y arrepentirse.
No poder con el miedo,
la cobardía,
el temor al sonido de la voz.
Huir como ciervo asustado del propio corazón,
vociferando un nombre en el silencio
y hacer ruido,
llenarse de otras voces,
sólo para seguirnos desgarrando
y aumentar el espanto
de haber perdido el cielo para siempre.

To spend days
lifting the hand to search
for the right welcoming gesture, then being sorry,
unable to master fear,
a lack of courage,
dreading the sound of a certain voice.
To flee like a deer frightened by its own heartbeat,
screaming a name in the silence
and making noise
to fill the internal void with other voices,
only to go on tearing each other apart
and increasing the fear
of having forfeited the sky forever.

In Memoriam

Como una inmensa catedral,
ahumada de tiempo y peregrinos,
abierta de vitrales,
cobijada de musgo y pequeñas violetas olorosas,
esta noche oficio para vos,
un *In Memoriam* cálido,
una lámpara ardiendo.

Por los más oscuros pasadizos de mis muros internos,
a través de intrincados laberintos,
de puertas canceladas,
de candados y rejas,
camino hacia el encuentro de tu sombra.
Tu efigie de largas vestiduras monacales
me espera en el atrio del recuerdo
junto a la fuente silenciada.

Arrastro las largas vestiduras del encierro.
No sé si notarás,
cuando callada te me acerque,
cómo mi corazón semeja un cirio
y cómo se me amontonan en los ojos
todas las mieles espesas de la sangre.

En el redondo espacio temporal
de esta noche en que invoco tu nombre,
alzo el manto que oculta quedamente el secreto,
te muestro el altar de los suspiros,
la caja cincelada donde guardo tus gestos,
el conjuro de rosas que perfuma mis huesos.

Mi cuerpo tu perenne habitación.
Tu morada de las suaves paredes.

In Memoriam

Like an immense cathedral,
filled with the incense of time and pilgrims,
my stained-glass windows open,
covered with moss and fragrant tiny violets,
ardently, tonight,
I celebrate for you
a burning *In Memoriam*.

Through the darkest corridors of my internal fortress,
crossing intricate labyrinths
doors boarded shut,
locks and bars,
I advance to encounter your shadow.
Dressed in long monastic robes,
your image awaits me in the atrium of memory
close to the silenced fountain.

I drag the long robes of confinement.
Perhaps you will not notice,
as I quietly approach you,
the way my heart resembles a ceremonial candle
and how blood and thick honey
rush together, melting in my eyes.

In the round, temporal space of this night,
where I invoke your name,
the veil is lifted that keeps the secret hidden.
I bestow upon you the altar of sighs,
the carved box where I guard your gestures,
the spell of roses that perfumes my bones.

Endlessly, you inhabit my body.
Your realm of soft borders.

Quizás ya no recuerdes
cómo ocupabas sus entrañas,
sus celdas enrejadas,
pero ellas conocen los murmullos, los cánticos.
Basta una chispa y lo muerto revive,
lo que pensábase dormido, despierta.

Oficio así esta resurrección,
este rito de invierno,
abierta, florecida como las limonarias.
Te enrostro mi amor enclaustrado,
sepultado tras días y barrotes de acero,
este amor sumergido tras pétalos de agua,
conservado en archivos subterráneos
lapidado, proscrito, negado miles veces,
intacto zarzal sin consumirse,
delicado reducto que la sangre preserva.
Lo pongo de nuevo en su lugar,
en su jaula del jardín de maduras manzanas,
lo condeno otra vez a la ceguera, lo silencio.

Ya mañana
trataré de olvidar
que, de luto, esta noche
me habitaste de nuevo
y fui aquella mujer que te llamaba
sin que jamás tu voz le respondiera.

Perhaps you don't remember
the caves you once possessed,
the rooms with barred windows.
But they remember the murmuring, the canticles.
Just one spark is needed to awaken what appeared to be dead,
what seemed to be asleep.

And so I celebrate this resurrection,
this rainy season ritual,
open, blossoming.
I scorn you with my cloistered love,
sealed under days and steel bars,
this love submerged under petals of water,
kept away in underground vaults,
buried alive, banned, denied a thousand times,
burning bush that never turns to ash,
delicate recess maintained by blood.
I return it to where it belongs,
to its cage in the garden of ripened apples,
again, I condemn it to blindness, I silence it.

When morning comes,
I will try to forget
that tonight, dressed in mourning,
you were in me again, and once more
I was that woman who used to call your name
when your voice never answered.

Mayo

No se marchitan los besos
como los malinches,
ni me crecen vainas en los brazos;
siempre florezco
con esta lluvia interna,
como los patios verdes de mayo
y río porque amo el viento y las nubes
y el paso de los pájaros cantores,
aunque ande enredada en recuerdos,
cubierta de hiedra como las viejas paredes,
sigo creyendo en los susurros guardados,
la fuerza de los caballos salvajes,
el alado mensaje de las gaviotas.

Creo en las raíces innumerables de mi canto.

May

Kisses don't wither
like the flowers of the *malinche* tree,
hard shells of seeds don't grow over my arms;
I'm always flowering
with this internal rain,
like the green patios in May
and I laugh because I love the wind and the clouds
and the singing birds passing overhead,
even though I'm entangled in memories,
covered with ivy like old walls,
I go on believing in the secret whisperings,
the strength of wild horses,
the winged message of gulls.

I believe in the countless roots of my song.

Si yo no viviera

Si yo no viviera en un país asediado
que rodeado de muerte nos da vida.

Si no creyera en la fuerza del pensamiento
y pensara que sólo es útil
para ejercicio del cerebro.

Si no me despertara cada mañana
con algo menos,
algo que ya no está:
— el jabón, las bujías, la leche —
y no supiera que en adelante
tendré que inventarme hasta la luz
y volver contenta
a lo primitivo y bueno
que hay en cada casa,
en cada corazón.

Si no caminara cotidianamente
en la navaja que separa las nubes
del cielo y el infierno
y fuera una mujer de lino en un país planchado
desarrollado
lleno de todo lo que aquí nos falta. . .

Seguramente
hubiera pasado a tu lado
sin mirarte
sin que me vieras.
Seguramente
ni vos
ni yo

If I Didn't Live

If I didn't live in a besieged country
that gives us life while surrounded by death.

If I didn't believe in the force of thought
and considered it good only
as exercise for the brain.

If I didn't wake up each morning
with a little less,
something that is no longer there —
soap, candles, milk —
and I didn't know that in the future
I may even have to invent light
and be content
with what's primitive and good
in every house,
in every heart.

If I didn't walk every day
on the blade that separates the clouds
of heaven and hell
and I were a woman dressed in fine linen
from a developed, dry-cleaned country,
with all the things that we're lacking here. . .

Most likely,
I would have walked by
without looking at you
without you seeing me.
Most likely,
neither you
nor I

estaríamos ahora sentados
mirándonos
tocándonos
acariciando
como a un niño
el tiempo.

would be sitting together now
looking at each other,
touching each other,
caressing
time
as if it were a child.

Pequeñas lecciones de erotismo I

I

Recorrer un cuerpo en su extensión de vela
Es dar la vuelta al mundo
Atravesar sin brújula la rosa de los vientos
Islas golfos penínsulas diques de aguas enbravecidas
No es tarea fácil — sí placentera —
No creas hacerlo en un día o noche de sábanas
    explayadas
Hay secretos en los poros para llenar muchas lunas

II

El cuerpo es carta astral en lenguaje cifrado
Encuentras un astro y quizá deberás empezar
Corregir el rumbo cuando nubehuracán o aullido profundo
Te pongan estremecimientos
Cuenco de la mano que no sospechaste

III

Repasa muchas veces una extensión
Encuentra el lago de los nenúfares
Acaricia con tu ancla el centro del lirio
Sumérgete ahógate distiéndete
No te niegues el olor la sal el azúcar
Los vientos profundos cúmulos nimbus de los pulmones
Niebla en el cerebro
Temblor de las piernas
Maremoto adormecido de los besos

Brief Lessons in Eroticism I

I

To sail the entire length of a body
Is to circle the world
To navigate the rose of the winds without a compass
Islands gulfs peninsulas breakwaters against crashing waves
It's not easy to find such pleasure
Don't think you can get it one day or night of consoling sheets
There are enough secrets in the pores to fill many moons

II

The body is an astral chart in a coded language
Find a star and perhaps you'll begin
To change course when suddenly a hurricane or piercing scream
Makes you tremble in fear
A crease in the hand you didn't expect

III

Go over the entire length many times
Find the lake with the white water lilies
Caress the lily's center with your anchor
Plunge deep drown yourself stretch your limbs
Don't deny yourself the smell the salt the sugar
The heavy winds cumulonimbus-lungs
The brain's dense fog
Earthquake of legs
Sleeping tidal wave of kisses

IV

Instálate en el humus sin miedo al desgaste sin prisa
No quieras alcanzar la cima
Retrasa la puerta del paraíso
Acuna tu ángel caído revuélvele la espesa cabellera con la
Espada de fuego usurpada
Muerde la manzana

V

Huele
Duele
Intercambia miradas saliva imprégnate
Da vueltas imprime sollozas piel que se escurre
Pie hallazgo al final de la pierna
Persíguelo busca secreto del paso forma del talón
Arco del andar bahías formando arqueado caminar
Gústalos

VI

Escucha caracola del oído
Cómo gime la humedad
Lóbulo que se acerca al labio sonido de la respiración
Poros que se alzan formando diminutas montañas
Sensación estremecida de piel insurrecta al tacto
Suave puente nuca desciende al mar pecho
Marea del corazón susúrrale
Encuentra la gruta del agua

IV

Place yourself in the humus without fear
     of wearing out there's no hurry
Delay reaching the peak
the threshold of paradise
Rock your fallen angel let your usurped sword of fire
lose itself in the thick hair
Bite the apple

V

Ocean smell
Pain as well
Exchange glances saliva impregnate yourself
Roll over imprint of sobs skin that slips away
Foot discovery at the end of the leg
Pursue it look for the secret of the passage the heel's shape
Arch of each footstep bays shaping arched stride
Taste them

VI

Listen to the shell of the ear
How the dampness moans
Earlobe approaching the lip sound of breathing
Pores that rise up to form tiny mountains
Shivery insurrection of skin caressed
Gentle bridge neck go down to the sea breast
The heart's tide whisper to her
Find the grotto of water

VII

Traspasa la tierra del fuego la buena esperanza
Navega loco en la juntura de los oceános
Cruza las algas ármate de corales ulula gime
Emerge con la rama de olivo llora socavando ternuras ocultas
Desnuda miradas de asombro
Despeña el sextante desde lo alto de la pestaña
Arquea las cejas abre ventanas de la nariz

VIII

Aspira suspira
Muérete un poco
Dulce lentamente muérete
Agoniza contra la pupila extiende el goce
Dobla el mástil hincha las velas
Navega dobla hacia Venus
estrella de la mañana
— el mar como un vasto cristal azogado —
duérmete náufrago.

VII

Cut through tierra del fuego good hope
Navigate the madness where the seas join
Sail over the algae arm yourself with coral howl moan
Emerge with the olive branch cry undermining
       all hidden tenderness
Let looks of astonishment go naked
Throw down the sextant from the heights of the eyelash
Arch your eyebrows open the nose's windows

VIII

Breathe in breathe out
Die a little
Sweetly slowly die
Come to death against the eye's center let the pleasure go on
Turn the rudder spread the sails
Sail on turn toward Venus
morning star
— the sea like a vast mercuric crystal —
sleep you shipwrecked sailor.

Pequeñas lecciones de erotismo II

I

Así como el más apacible estanque
puede quebrar el cambiante reflejo del cielo
cuando la más leve brizna de hierba o viento
lo conmueven
y nunca repetirse
así la suave piel que te refleja
puede deshacerse en círculos concéntricos
la pierna tornarse ala con un leve toque
volar olvidada de Newton y sus manzanas
aparecer detrás del cuello
o apuntar al cielo
como brazo de una antigua estatua.

II

Rasgado el velo
cuando todo se asiente
cual líquida extendida plataforma
busca los pensamientos
el cáliz de las sensaciones
el retorcido laberinto blanco de los lóbulos
la división de los hemisferios
la cúpula ósea haciendo y deshaciendo
la copa del árbol
hunde tus dedos en la maraña vegetal
atraviesa las hebras
imagínate las doradas crines del maíz
reposa tu mano en esa dura redondez
donde toda filosofía se aloja
donde todo lo que de ti se ama está registrado

Brief Lessons in Eroticism II

I

Just as the most peaceful pond
can shatter the sky's changing reflection
when the slightest blade of grass or wind
stirs it
never to repeat itself
so the soft skin that reflects you
can become concentric circles
the leg can change into a wing at the slightest touch
fly with no memory of Newton and his apples
appear behind the neck
or aim for the sky
like the arm from an ancient statue.

II

Once the veil is torn
when everything settles
like an extended liquid platform
look for the thoughts
the chalice of sensations
the ears' twisted white labyrinth
the separation of the hemispheres
the bone cupola making and unmaking
the treetop
sink your fingers into the dense undergrowth
move through each fiber
imagine the golden tassles of corn
rest your hand on that hard roundness
where all philosophy makes its home
where everything loved about you is registered

¿No querrás acariciar la infancia desgarbada?
¿Aquel recuerdo, aquella tarde?
¿El secreto que acaso aún te guarda?
Deslízate por los delgados pasillos
pon tus táctiles yemas hondo
asiéntate en el centro de los destellos

III

Acércate despacio
al otro lado de la luna
la clara llanura
la sien frente donde rueda el ceño
despliega el manifiesto del gozo
ábrete a la serena acuosidad del iris
húndete en el fondo de la transparencia
mírate
bébete Narciso tu amante amada imagen
besa
hasta espesar el agua.

Don't you want to caress graceless infancy
That distant memory, that afternoon?
The secret that perhaps still keeps you?
Slide down the thin passageways
touch deep with your fingertips
put yourself in the center of the sparkling.

III

Come closer slowly
on the far side of the moon
the clear plain
the temple forehead where the brow wheels —
unfurl the manifesto of pleasure
open yourself to the serene waters of the iris
plunge to the bottom of transparency
look at yourself
drink your lover Narcissus beloved image
kiss
until the water is still.

Nicaragua agua fuego

Lluvia
Ventana trae agua sobre hojas
viento pasa arrastrando faldas
lodos llevan troncos
árboles pintan estrellas charcos de sangre
fronteras de un día que hay que pelear
sin remedio sin más alternativa que la lucha
Detrás de cortina mojada
escribo dedos sobre gatillos
guerras grandes
dolores tamaño ojos de madres
goteando aguaceros incontenibles
vienen los cuerpecitos helados muertos
bajan de la montaña los muchachos
con sus hamacas recuperadas de la contra
comemos poco hay poco queremos comer todos
manos grandes blancas quieren matarnos
pero hicimos hospitales camas
donde mujeres gritan nacimientos
todo el día pasamos palpitando
tum tum tam tam
venas de indios repiten historia:
No queremos hijos que sean esclavos
flores salen de ataúdes
nadie muere en Nicaragua
Nicaragua mi amor mi muchachita violada
levantándose componiéndose la falda
caminando detrás del asesino siguiéndolo
montaña abajo montaña arriba
no pasarán dicen los pajaritos
no pasarán dicen los amantes que hacen el amor
que hacen hijos que hacen pan que hacen trincheras

Nicaragua Water Fire

Rain
Window view of water on leaves
wind passes swishing skirts
muddy waters uproot tree trunks
trees paint stars puddles of blood
borders of a day that must be fought
there's no other way no alternative but the struggle
Behind curtains of water
I write fingers on triggers
great wars
suffering the size of mothers' eyes
dripping uncontainable cloudbursts
here come the small cold corpses
los muchachos come down from the mountains
with hammocks they recovered from the contras
we don't eat much there isn't much we all want to eat
big white hands want to kill us
but we made hospitals beds
where women scream births
all day we beat like hearts
tum tum tam tam
Indians' veins repeat history:
We don't want children who will be slaves
flowers blossom from coffins
no one dies in Nicaragua
Nicaragua my love my raped child
getting up straightening her skirt
walking behind the murderer following him
down the mountain up the mountain
they will not pass say the birds
they will not pass say the couples who make love
who make children who make bread who make trenches

que hacen uniformes que hacen cartas para los movilizados
Nicaragua mi amor mi negra miskita suma rama
palo de mayo en la laguna de Perlas
vientos huracanados bajando San Juan abajo
no pasarán y llueve sobre los sombreritos
que andan husmeando el rastro de las bestias
y no les dan descanso los persiguen los sacan
del pecho de la patria los arrancan sacan la hierba mala
no la dejan que pegue
queremos maíz arroz frijoles
que peguen las semillas en las tierras donde
campesino guarda en caja de madera título de Reforma Agraria
no pasen los diablos anunciando la buena nueva del perdón
a los que vieron ranchos arder
y vecino asesinado frente a su mujer y sus hijos
Nicaragua mi muchachita
baila sabe leer platica con la gente
le cuenta su cuento sale en aviones a contar su cuento
anda por todo el mundo con su cuento a tuto
habla hasta por los codos en periódicos de
        idiomas incomprensibles
grita se pone brava furiosa
parece mentira cuánta bulla mete y cómo resiste
aviones minas pirañas bombas maldiciones en inglés
discursos sobre cómo bajar la cabeza
y no se deja se suelta pega carreras
y allá va el General y la colina los cohetes reactivos
las columnas verdes avanzando despalando
haciendo ingenios de azúcar
ríos de leche casas escuelas
chavalos contando su historia
renqueando salidos del hospital
agarrando bus para volver al norte
viento que se sacude el miedo
nacimos para esto
reímos por esto

who make uniforms who write letters for the mobilized troops
Nicaragua my love my Black girl Miskito Sumo Rama
Maypole dance in Pearl Lagoon
hurricane winds blowing down the San Juan River
they will not pass and it rains on the young soldiers
tracking the scent of the beasts
never letting them rest following them pursuing them
uprooting them from the motherland's breast ripping them
        out like weeds
never letting them strike
we want corn rice beans
seeds taking root in the land
where a *campesino* keeps his Land Reform title in a wooden box
don't let the devils pass to announce the coming salvation
to the people who saw farms burn
and a neighbor murdered in front of his wife and children
Nicaragua my child
she dances she's learned to read to talk with people
to tell them her story to get on planes to tell her story
to travel around the world telling her story to everyone
speaking tirelessly in newspapers written in
        incomprehensible languages
screaming getting angry furious
all the noise she makes seems incredible so does the way she resists
planes mines speedboats bombs curses in English
speeches on how to bow one's head
and she fights breaks free flees
and there goes General Sandino and the hill the rocket launchers
the green columns advancing clearing land
building sugar mills
rivers of milk houses schools
young men telling their story
limping from the hospital
taking a bus to return to the north
wind that shakes fear
we were born for this
we rejoice for this

entre dientes andamos la rabia y la esperanza
no nos dejan no los dejamos ni a sol ni a sombra
país chiquito pero cumplidor
Nicaragua lanza lanzada atrevida chúcara yegua
potreros de Chontales donde Nadine
sueña caballos percherones
y soñamos en surtidor
tenemos una fábrica de sueños
sueños en serie para los descreídos
aquí nadie sale sin su arañazo en la conciencia
nadie pasa sin que le pase nada
país de locos iluminados poetas pintores
chorros de luces escuelas de danza
conferencias internacionales salones de protocolo
policías escolares regañando dulcemente
carne y hueso de gente que acierta y se equivoca
que prueba y vuelve a probar
aquí todo se mueve caderas de mujer bailando
sonando ganas de vivir ante momias
hablando de la muerte queriendo ganar su pasaje de regreso
en hojas impresas que salen por la tarde con sus mentiras
y sus rabias de histérica frustrada
envidia de la muchacha que se contonea, se chiquea,
cierra el ojo vende tamales vende pinturas
hace milicias va al parque inventa el amor
enciende los malinches se esconde para desconcertar
sale andando en medio de bayonetas caladas
hace circo y ferias y reza
y cree en la vida y en la muerte
y alista espadas de fuego
para que a nadie le quede más decisión
que paraíso terrenal
o cenizas
patria libre
o morir.

rage and hope clenched between our teeth
no rest for us no rest for them day or night
tiny but stubborn country
Nicaragua fearless spear daring wild mare
pastures in Chontales where Nadine
dreams of Percheron horses
and we have a fountain of dreams
we have a factory of dreams
a dream assembly line for the unbelievers
here no one gets away without a scratched conscience
no one comes here without being moved
country of enlightened lunatics poets painters
showers of lights schools dance
international conferences protocol
school-age police sweetly scolding
flesh and blood of people who sometimes are right
              sometimes make mistakes
who try and try again
everything moves here a dancing woman's hips
singing out a lust for life against the mummies
speaking of death hoping to earn their return trips
on printed pages that come out in the afternoon with their lies
and their rage of frustrated hysteria
envy of the girl who sways as she walks
winks sells tamales sells nail polish
joins the militia goes to the park invents love
sets the flowers of the *malinche* tree on fire hides to bewilder
comes out marching amidst drawn bayonets
sets up the circus and fairs and prays
and believes in life and death
and prepares swords of fire
so that the only choice can be
earthly paradise
or ashes
patria libre
o morir.

91

Acontecio en
un viaje de domingo a la playa

Llovía.
Nosotros pensábamos optimistas:
El camino se aclarará más adelante.
Seguramente en la playa, el sol.

El parabrisas del carro zas zas.
Neblina en las ventanas.
Arboles envueltos en sábanas blancas.
Gente mojada.
Frío en la carretera.

— Mejor estaríamos en la cama.
El horizonte hacia el lado del mar está todo nebuloso.
Devolvámonos a leer y abrazarnos. —

Giramos:
Entramos a Diriamba.
Todo el pueblo encerrado
guardado de la bruma la llovizna.

En el enredo de las esquinas
desembocamos de improviso en una rotonda:
Un monumento nombres de compañeros.
El cementerio al fondo.
Se veía hermoso.
Niebla suavizando la muerte.

— Bajemos. Nunca he estado aquí.
Quisiera ver la tumba de Ricardo Morales.
Dejarle algunas caricias sobre la tierra.
Unas hojitas de limonaria. —

It Happened on
a Sunday Trip to the Beach

It was raining.
We were optimistic:
it would be clear farther down the road,
sunny, for sure, at the beach.

The swish, swish of the windshield wipers.
Foggy windows.
Trees wrapped in white sheets.
People soaked to the skin.
Cold on the highway.

— We'd be better off in bed.
The horizon over the sea is thick with clouds.
Let's go back and read and embrace each other —

We turned.
Entered Diriamba.
The whole city locked
in mist and light rain.

In a maze of streets
we suddenly found ourselves at a traffic circle:
A monument, names of comrades.
The cemetery in the background.
It looked beautiful.
Fog softening death.

— Let's get out. I've never been here.
I've always wanted to see the grave of Ricardo Morales
and leave him a gentle message:
a few leaves from a lemon tree —

Bajamos.
Las tumbas de los ricos imponentes a la entrada.
Sus ángeles llorando lágrimas de lluvia.
Llovizna y tumbas buscando a Ricardo.
¿Dónde estará Ricardo?
Y encontramos lápidas de otros:
combatientes, padres, hermanos, monjas, octogenarias.
Hasta una mezquita oriental con este epitafio:
"Aquí yace Ramón López
que murió joven
disfrazado de anciano."
Pensamos en la muerte.
Yo, Ricardo, buscaba tus ojos.
Aquellos que unas pocas veces vi, inolvidables.
Los ojos de tu hija, Doris María.

No te encontramos.
Regresamos bajo la llovizna pertinaz.
Fue como tocar la puerta de tu casa y no hallarte.
Como que alguien dijera que habías salido,
que andabas en alguna reunión.
Fue como saber que tu tumba no existe,
que andás por allí,
apurado entre las calles mojadas
trabajando sin morirte nunca.

We got out.
The imposing graves of the rich at the entrance.
Their angels crying tears of rain.
Light rain and graves as we searched for Ricardo.
Where could Ricardo be?
And we found the gravestones of others:
combatants, fathers, brothers, nuns, eighty-year-olds.
Even a mosque from the East that bore this epitaph:
"Here lies Ramón López
who died young
disguised as an old man."
We thought about death.
As for me, Ricardo, I was looking for your eyes.
The unforgettable ones I saw just a few times.
The eyes of your daughter, Doris María.

We didn't find you.
We left under the persistent rain.
It was like knocking on your door and you weren't at home.
Like someone telling us you had gone out,
that you were at some meeting.
It was like knowing your grave doesn't exist,
that you're out there,
walking quickly through the wet streets,
working without ever dying.

Los portadores de sueños

En todas las profecías
está escrita la destrucción del mundo.

Todas las profecías cuentan
que el hombre creará su propia destrucción.

Pero los siglos y la vida que siempre se renueva
engendraron también una generación de amadores y soñadores;
hombres y mujeres que no soñaron con la destrucción del mundo,
sino con la construcción del mundo de las mariposas
y los ruiseñores.

Desde pequeños venían marcados por el amor.
Detrás de su apariencia cotidiana
guardaban la ternura y el sol de medianoche.
Sus madres los encontraban llorando por un pájaro muerto
y más tarde también los encontraron a muchos
muertos como pájaros.

Estos seres cohabitaron con mujeres traslúcidas
y las dejaron preñadas de miel y de hijos reverdecidos
por un invierno de caricias.

Así fue como proliferaron en el mundo los portadores de sueños,
atacados ferozmente por los portadores de profecías habladoras
de catástrofes.
Los llamaron ilusos, románticos, pensadores de utopías,
dijeron que sus palabras eran viejas
— y, en efecto, lo eran porque la memoria del paraíso es antigua
en el corazón del hombre —
los acumuladores de riquezas las temían
y lanzaban sus ejércitos contra ellos,

The Dream Bearers

In all the prophecies
the destruction of the world is written.

All the prophecies foretell
humanity creating its own destruction.

But time and life endlessly renewed
also engendered a generation of lovers and dreamers;
men and women who dreamt not of the world's destruction,
but of building a world of butterflies
and nightingales.

From an early age, they were branded by love.
Behind their everyday appearance
they hid tenderness and the midnight sun.
Their mothers often found them crying over a dead bird
and years later, found many of them
dead, too, like birds.

These beings lived with translucid women
and left them impregnated with honey and children
who grew like grass under the caress of rainy days.

This is how the dream bearers multiplied in the world,
fiercely attacked by those who bore catastrophic prophecies.
They were called deluded romantics, inventors of utopias.
They were told their words were old —
which was true, since paradise has been an ancient memory
in the heart of humanity.
Those who accumulated riches feared them,
and hurled their armies against them.

pero los portadores de sueños todas las noches hacían el amor
y seguía brotando su semilla del vientre de ellas
que no sólo portaban sueños sino que los multiplicaban
y los hacían correr y hablar.

De esta forma el mundo engendró de nuevo su vida
como también había engendrado a los que inventaron la manera
de apagar el sol.

Los portadores de sueños sobrevivieron a los climas gélidos
pero en los climas cálidos casi parecían brotar por
        generación espontánea.
Quizá las palmeras, los cielos azules, las lluvias torrenciales
tuvieron algo que ver con esto,
la verdad es que como laboriosas hormiguitas
estos especímenes no dejaban de soñar y de construir
        hermosos mundos,
mundos de hermanos, de hombres y mujeres que se
        llamaban compañeros,
que se enseñaban unos a otros a leer, se consolaban en las muertes,
se curaban y cuidaban entre ellos, se querían, se ayudaban en el
arte de querer y en la defensa de la felicidad.

Eran felices en su mundo de azúcar y viento
y de todas partes venían a impregnarse de su aliento
y de sus claras miradas
y hacia todas partes salían los que los habían conocido
portando sueños
soñando con profecías nuevas
que hablaban de tiempos de mariposas y ruiseñores
en que el mundo no tendría que terminar en la hecatombe
y, por el contrario, los científicos diseñarían
fuentes, jardines, juguetes sorprendentes
para hacer más gozosa la felicidad del hombre.

But every night the dream bearers made love,
and their seed continued growing in the wombs
of women who not only bore dreams but multiplied them,
and made them run and speak.

This is how the world engendered its life again
just as it had engendered those who invented the way
to extinguish the sun.

The dream bearers survived the cold climates,
but in the warm climates they seemed to sprout
        by spontaneous generation.
Perhaps the palm trees, the blue skies, the torrential rains
had something to do with this.
The truth is that these specimens, like hard-working little ants,
never stopped dreaming and building their beautiful worlds,
worlds of brothers and sisters, of men and women who called
        each other *compañeros*,
who taught each other to read, consoled each other
        in times of death,
healed and cared for each other, loved and helped each other
in the art of loving and in the defense of happiness.

They were happy in their world of sugar and wind
and people came from all directions to be impregnated
        by their breath
and by their clear gazes
and the people who had known them
went out in all directions
bearing dreams
dreaming new prophecies
that spoke of times of butterflies and nightingales
in which the world would not have to end up in a hecatomb.
On the contrary, scientists would design
fountains, gardens, surprising toys
to further humanity's happiness.

Son peligrosos — imprimían las grandes rotativas
Son peligrosos — decían los presidentes en sus discursos
Son peligrosos — murmuraban los artífices de la guerra

Hay que destruirlos — imprimían las grandes rotativas
Hay que destruirlos — decían los presidentes en sus discursos
Hay que destruirlos — murmuraban los artífices de la guerra.

Los portadores de sueños conocían su poder
y por eso no se extrañaban.
Y también sabían que la vida los había engendrado
para protegerse de la muerte que anuncian las profecías.
Y por eso defendían su vida aun con la muerte.
Y por eso cultivaban jardines de sueños
y los exportaban con grandes lazos de colores
y los profetas de la oscuridad se pasaban noches y días enteros
vigilando los pasajes y los caminos
buscando estos peligrosos cargamentos
que nunca lograban atrapar
porque el que no tiene ojos para soñar
no ve los sueños ni de día, ni de noche.

Y en el mundo se ha desatado un gran tráfico de sueños
que no pueden detener los traficantes de la muerte;
y por doquier hay paquetes con grandes lazos
que sólo esta nueva raza de hombres puede ver
y la semilla de estos sueños no se puede detectar
porque va envuelta en rojos corazones
o en amplios vestidos de maternidad
donde piesecitos soñadores alborotan los vientres que los cargan.

Dicen que la tierra después de parirlos
desencadenó un cielo de arco iris
y sopló de fecundidad las raíces de los árboles.

They are dangerous read the message that rolled off the presses
They are dangerous said the presidents in their speeches
They are dangerous murmured the makers of war

They must be destroyed read the message that rolled off
       the presses
They must be destroyed said the presidents in their speeches
They must be destroyed murmured the makers of war.

The dream bearers knew their power
and therefore were not surprised.
And they also knew that life had engendered them
to protect itself from the death announced in the prophecies.
And so they defended their lives even with death.
And so they cultivated gardens of dreams
and exported them tied with big colorful ribbons
and the prophets of darkness spent days and nights
watching the secret routes and the roads
searching for these dangerous shipments
which they never succeeded in intercepting
because the person with no eyes for dreaming
cannot see dreams either by day or night.

And in the world a dream-traffic has been unleashed
that the traffickers in death cannot stop;
and everywhere there are packages with big bows
that only this new race of people can see,
and the seed of these dreams cannot be detected
because it is enclosed in red hearts
or in ample maternity dresses
where tiny feet of dreamers teem inside the wombs that bear them.

It is said that earth, after giving birth to them,
unchained a rainbow in the sky
and blew the breath of fertility on the roots of trees.

Nosotros sólo sabemos que los hemos visto
Sabemos que la vida los engendró
para protegerse de la muerte que anuncian las profecías.

All we know is that we have seen them
We know that life engendered them
as protection against the prophecies of death.

Nueva York

Bosque de los huracanes
Se aproxima la ciudad de las altas chimeneas
Es Nueva York
Nueva York
Las nubes se enredan en la cresta de la ciudad
Desde arriba las calles semejan rejas
de un inmenso acerado laberinto
Se levanta la humareda el vaho el vapor
espuma de gente que vive
olas de seres batiéndose en marea baja y marea alta
en las costas calles contra las rocas picos rascacielos
Corre el avión sobre rampas lisas rectas
bulbos azules blancos señalan la pista de aterrizaje
Bajamos a la ciudad de los tumultos
nudo de las aglomeraciones
ruido de trenes buses taxis
rostros innumerables
rostros vistos una sola vez
irrepetibles consumidos en la profundidad
moviéndose hacia destinos desconocidos
maletas etiquetas evocando países remotos
coincidimos en la hilera abordando los taxis amarillos
nos separamos sin saber quiénes somos
todos vamos a alguna parte
sin mirarnos
cuerpos apretados cuerpos que chocan
ojos que no se encuentran
Entramos corremos surcamos autopistas iluminadas
puentes arcos el río oscuro corriendo abandonado a su suerte
como nosotros
como todos aquí archipiélagos islas sin puentes
cruzando puentes artificiosamente labrados en el acero

New York

Forest of hurricanes
The city of high chimneys looms
It's New York
New York
The clouds are tangled in the city's crest
From the air the streets resemble the grates
of an immense labyrinth of steel
Rising smoke mist steam
surf of living people
waves of beings crashing at low tide and high tide
against coasts streets against the rocks cliffs skyscrapers
The plane flies over smooth straight ramps
blue white lights mark the runway
We descend into the city of tumult
knot of conglomerations
noise of trains buses taxis
countless faces
faces seen only once
unrepeatable consumed in the profundity
moving toward unknown fates
suitcases labels evoking remote countries
we meet in the line of people hailing yellow cabs
we separate without knowing who we are
we're all going somewhere
without looking at each other
bodies pressed together bodies bumping into each other
eyes that never meet
We enter we speed we plow our way down brightly-lit highways
bridges arches the dark river flowing abandoned to its fate
like us
like everyone here archipelagos islands without bridges
crossing bridges of elaborately decorated steel

Nueva York
vieja bruja fascinante cambiante camaleón
caja de pandora abiertas calles abiertas faldas
abiertas puertas hacia la tentación
libros muebles ropa revistas restaurantes tiendas
tiendas tiendas caras baratas cines teatros modas
deportes pornografía zapatos queso sorbete
conciertos ópera boutiques almacenes inmensos
el almacén más grande del mundo
pisos pisos pisos unos sobre los otros
cafeterías hamburguesas supermercados
salmón ostras aguacates jugo de naranja
máquinas para jugar para excitarse para pensar
para calcular drogas para soñar
audífonos para pasear por las calles
oyendo música en patines surcando navegando
ausente de la calle los transeúntes pasando
Nueva York
de altos edificios gemelos
los más altos del mundo: el World Trade Building
el edificio del comercio dominando toda la ciudad
Dios de la ciudad
dos torres dos ojos mirando
Bosque de los huracanes
Tantos árboles de concreto tantas ventanas altas
Cuando el viento sopla se crean corrientes furiosas
enorme boca soplando su propio clima
ventiscas atizadas por los rascacielos
el viento atrapado en esta red gigante
nacida de la mano del hombre
Nueva York
aquí trabajaron trabajan miles de personas
dejaron dejan sus años sus sueños
engendraron engendran hijos
levantaron levantan estas columnas atrapadoras de nubes
puertos aeropuertos estaciones carreteras

106

New York
fascinating old witch changing chameleon
Pandora's box open streets open skirts
doors open to temptation
books furniture clothes magazines restaurants
expensive stores cheap stores stores cinemas theatres fashion
sports pornography shoes cheese sherbet
concerts opera boutiques immense department stores
the biggest department store in the world
floor after floor after floor one on top of the other
cafeterias hamburgers supermarkets
salmon oysters avocados orange juice
machines for play for excitement for thinking for calculating
drugs for dreaming
headphones for walking down the streets
listening to music on roller skates making their way navigating
absent from the street among all the passersby
New York
with its high twin buildings
the world's tallest: The World Trade Center
the commercial building dominating the entire city
God of the city
two towers two eyes watching
Forest of hurricanes
So many concrete trees so many high windows
The wind blows furious gusts
enormous mouth blowing its own climate
blizzards stirred by skyscrapers
the wind trapped in this gigantic net
born from humanity's hand
New York
here thousands of people worked work
they left leave behind their years their dreams
they engendered engender children
they lifted lift these columns that trap the clouds
ports airports stations highways

aviones trenes barcos trajeron griegos irlandeses
italianos chinos hindúes árabes latinos polacos
rusos japoneses filipinos africanos
buscadores de fortunas perseguidos esclavos
exiliados aventureros músicos poetas
científicos locos gangsters anónimos inmigrantes
olas de rostros confundidos desleídos perdidos
Aquí vive un pueblo
un árbol de muchas raíces
vidas muertes de quienes aquí se entendieron
socios de la soledad y el estrépito
Nueva York
Central Park
Se nos acercan las ardillas
Es raro que se acerquen pero las llamé les hablé
Vinieron miedosas caminando sobre la grama yerta por el invierno
Troncos lisos sin hojas
desnudos esqueléticos hermosos en el atardecer del frío
Jóvenes jugando base-ball parejas abrazadas
nosotros abrazados confundidos
caminando sin rostros sin identidad para nadie
granos de arena en esta playa tumulto del anonimato
Muelles de Nueva York
el río corriendo el Hudson derramándose
estirando su tira plateada robles negros
recortados en el atardecer el hombre paseando sus perros
el homosexual llamando al teléfono público
preguntando por el amado
clavos herrumbados maderos carcomidos por el agua
arañazos de aviones serpenteando el cielo congestionado
miles de aviones todo el día entrando y saliendo
trenes subterráneos
mundo subterráneo atronador carriles estaciones
vagones pintados de consignas que no dicen nada
pintas en las paredes ininteligibles
signos de quienes no saben qué decir

planes trains boats brought Greek Irish
Italians Chinese Hindus Arabs Latinos Polish
Russians Japanese Filipinos Africans
fortune-seekers runaways slaves
the exiled the adventurers musicians poets
scientists crazies gangsters anonymous immigrants
waves of confused dissolved lost faces
Here a people lives
a tree with many roots
lives deaths of those who managed to understand each other here
partners in loneliness and deafening noise
New York
Central Park
The squirrels come close to us
It's strange for them to come so close but I called them spoke to them
They came frightened walking on the grass stiff with winter
Smooth trunks with no leaves
naked skeletons beautiful in the afternoon cold
Kids playing baseball couples embracing
like us embraced confused
walking with no faces no identity for anyone
grains of sand on this beach tumult of anonymity
Docks of New York
the flowing river the Hudson spilling over its banks
stretching out its silver strip black oaks
outlined in the afternoon the man walking his dogs
the homosexual calling on the public telephone
asking for his lover
Rusted spikes wood eaten away by the water
claw marks of planes crisscrossing the congested sky
thousands of planes all day long landing and taking off
subways
deafening underground world tracks stations
subway cars painted with slogans that mean nothing
unintelligible spray-painted messages on the walls
signs of those who don't know what to say

sólo que quieren decir algo confuso
dejar huella llamar la atención armados
de latas de pintura emborronando el aluminio
corriéndose de la policía
violando matando sirenas a todas horas
pleitos callejeros insultos salidos de cualquier parte
Rostros vivos muertos alegres tristes
personas que quieren platicar comunicarse
hablarse entre sí los incomunicados
la mujer gritando en la calle
por Dios ayúdenme — en español —
pasando a su lado nadie se detiene
Se van a sus casas toman café
café mañana tarde y noche
café traído de países como el nuestro
países pequeños pobres exportadores de café
países que toman café aguado para que en Nueva York
pasemos por tiendas donde el café empapa el olor de toda la calle
Nueva York
Vieja bruja fascinante
Puta cara carísima vida carísima comida carísimos libros
apartamentos carísimos
Gozar es tener dinero
Sólo necesitás dinero
Sin dinero no hacés nada
Bancos sacrosantos semejando confesionarios
con máquinas códigos dispensadores de dinero
apretás un número y salen los billetes
Entran las personas a retirar dinero
Unas al lado de las otras respetuosas
no se miran diríase que están rezando
Nueva York
Bosque de los huracanes
Bella ciudad horrible
pobre gente rica pobre gente pobre
fascinación hechizo magia de la abundancia

only that they want to say something confusing
to leave a trail to get some attention armed
with cans of spray paint scribbling on the aluminum
running from the police
raping killing
sirens at all hours arguments in the street insults bursting
        from nowhere
Living dead happy sad faces
people who want to chat to communicate
to speak amongst each other — the incommunicados
the woman screaming in the street in Spanish
Por Dios ayúdenme For God's sake help me
passing by her no one stops
They go home and drink coffee
coffee morning noon and night
coffee brought from countries like ours
small poor countries that export coffee
countries that drink watered down coffee so that in New York
we pass by stores where the smell of coffee fills the street
New York
Old fascinating witch
Expensive whore exorbitant life exorbitant food books apartments
To enjoy is to have money
All you need is money
Without money you can't do anything
Sacrosanct banks resembling confessionals
with coded machines that dispense money
you punch in a number and out come the bills
People go in to withdraw money
politely standing next to each other
without looking at each other as if in prayer
New York
Forest of hurricanes
Beautiful horrible city
poor rich people poor poor people
fascination magical spell of abundance

olas de seres batiéndose en marea alta y marea baja
felices desgraciados seres humanos
apretujados en este vientre contráctil
ciudad vomitándolos naciéndolos
seres abigarrados enrejados pegados unos a los otros
rehuyéndose los ojos huyendo a sus pequeños mundos
cuidando luchando para que no se les confunda el nombre
la identidad conocer su ventana en la maraña de pisos
no perder la llave la casa el trabajo la mujer el hombre
la lágrima el tacto el semen
sobrevivir
sobrevivir como nosotros que sobrevivimos
que luchamos para sobrevivirlos a ellos que sobreviven
Nueva York
Bosque de los huracanes

Mañana aterrizaremos en Aeropuerto Augusto César Sandino
y la ruta la pista el aterrizaje estará iluminado por candiles
pequeños pobres cientos de candiles.

waves of beings crashing at low tide and high tide
happy wretched human beings
squeezed together in this contracting womb
city vomiting them giving birth to them
tangled mix of people stuck to each other
glances never meeting fleeing to their own little worlds
taking care struggling so as not to confuse their name
their identity to know which window is theirs in the tangled
          growth of multi-storied buildings
not to lose the key the home the job the wife the husband
the tear the sense of touch the semen
to survive
to survive the way we survive
we who struggle to survive the very people who survive
New York
Forest of hurricanes

Tomorrow we'll land at Augusto César Sandino Airport
and the route the runway the landing will be lit by oil lamps
hundreds of small primitive oil lamps.

Conjunción

Afuera
la noche agazapada
aguarda como tigre
el salto mortal a través de la ventana;
en este recinto donde doliosamente
hago surgir del aire las palabras
me asombra la latente presencia de un beso sobre la pierna.
No hay nadie: sólo mi cuerpo solo,
mi cuerpo y los cabellos extendidos en imágenes
estoy yo y están ellas
las mujeres sin habla
esas que mis dedos alumbran
esas que la noche se lleva en su aliento de luna.

Mujeres de los siglos me habitan:
Isadora bailando con su túnica
Virginia Woolf, su cuarto propio
Safo lanzándose desde la roca;
Medea, Fedra, Jane Eyre
y mis amigas
espantando lo viejo del tiempo
escribiéndose a sí mismas
sacudiendo las sombras para alumbrar sus perfiles
y dejarse ver por fin
desnudadas de toda convención.

Mujeres danzan a la luz de mi lámpara
se suben a las mesas, dicen discursos incendiarios
me sitian con los sufrimientos
las marcas del cuerpo el alumbramiento de los hijos
el silencio de las olorosas cocinas los
efímeros tensos dormitorios.

Conjunction

Outside
the crouching night
waits like a tiger
the mortal leap through the window
within these walls where painfully
I make the words emerge from the air,
the latent presence of a kiss on my leg surprises me.
There is no one. Only my body alone.
My body and my hair extended in images.
I am here and so are they
the speechless women
the ones my fingers illuminate
the ones the night's moon-breath carries.

Women of the centuries inhabit me:
Isadora dancing with her tunic
Virginia Woolf, a room of her own,
Sappho throwing herself from the rock;
Medea, Phaedra, Jane Eyre
and my women-friends
scaring time's aging
writing themselves
shaking off the shadows to pour light on their faces
and being seen at last
stripped of all convention.

Women dance by the light of my lamp,
climb onto the tables, give incendiary speeches
besiege me with their suffering
the bruises on their bodies the pain of childbirth
the silence of the fragrant kitchens
the ephemeral tense bedrooms.

Mujeres enormes monumentos me circundan
dicen sus poemas cantan bailan recuperan la voz;
dicen: No pude estudiar latín: no pude
escribir como Shakespeare;
nadie se apiadó de mi gusto por la música;
George Sand: tuve que disfrazarme de hombre;
escribí oculta en el nombre masculino.
Y más allá Jane Austen, acomodando las
palabras de "Orgullo y Prejuicio"
en un cuaderno en la sala común de la parroquia
interrumpida innumerablemente por los visitantes.

Mujeres de los siglos adustas envejecidas tiernas
con los ojos brillantes descienden a mi entorno
ellas perecederas inmortales
parecieran gozar detrás de las pestañas
viendo mi cuarto propio
el nítido legajo de papeles blancos
el moderno electrónico computador
los estantes de libros
los gruesos diccionarios
el cenicero negro de ceniza
el humo del cigarro.

Yo miro los armarios con la ropa blanca
las pequeñas y suaves prendas íntimas
la lista del mercado en la mesa de noche;
siento la necesidad de un beso sobre la pierna.

Great women monumental women encircle me
they recite their poems sing dance win back their voices;
they say: I couldn't study Latin: I couldn't
write like Shakespeare;
no one took pity on my love for music;
George Sand: I had to disguise myelf as a man;
I wrote hidden behind a masculine name.
And beyond, Jane Austen placing the
words of "Pride and Prejudice"
in a notebook in the common room of the parish
endlessly interrupted by visitors.

Sober, aged, gentle women of the centuries,
with shining eyes, come down to surround me
these perishable immortal women
glance around my room with pleasure:
the neat pile of white paper
the modern electronic word processor
the shelves of books
the thick dictionaries
the ashtray black with ashes
the cigarette smoke.

I look at the linen closet
the soft and silky underwear in the drawer
the shopping list on the night table;
I still feel like I need a kiss on my leg.

Biographical Notes

Gioconda Belli

was born in Managua, Nicaragua in 1948. At age fourteen, she left Nicaragua to finish high school in Spain. After high school, she studied advertising in Philadelphia and then returned to Nicaragua when she was eighteen and got married. She worked as an account executive in advertising until she became actively involved in the political struggle to overthrow the Somoza dictatorship. By this time she had also started to write poetry, and her first book *Sobre la grama* (*On the Grass*), 1974, won her the most prestigious literary prize awarded by the Nicaraguan National University, the Mariano Fiallos Gil Prize.

Because of her ties to the national liberation movement, Gioconda Belli had to go into exile in 1975. She lived in Costa Rica for three years with her two daughters. In Costa Rica, she also gave birth to her son, Camilo, and finished a second book of poetry, *Línea de fuego* (*Line of Fire*), for which she received the Casa de las Américas Prize in 1978.

After the revolutionary triumph in Nicaragua, she returned to her homeland. She held several important positions both in the government and in the party structures until 1986, when she began writing a novel and decided to dedicate her time to her work as a writer. Her poetry books *Truenos y arco iris* (*Thunder and Rainbow*) and *De la costilla de Eva* (*From Eve's Rib*) appeared in 1982 and 1986 respectively. In 1985, an anthology of her poetry was published: *Amor insurrecto* (*Insurrectional Love*).

Her first novel, *La mujer habitada* (*The Inhabited Woman*) was published in both Nicaragua and Germany in 1988. The German edition was awarded the Prize of the Best Literary Work of the Year by the Union of German Publishers and Editors.

At present Gioconda Belli lives in Managua, Nicaragua with her husband Charles Castaldi.

Steven F. White

was born in Abington, Pennsylvania in 1955 and was raised in Glencoe, Illinois. He was educated at Williams College and the University of Oregon. He has traveled and worked in many Latin American countries, including Nicaragua in 1979. He received a Fulbright grant in 1983 to translate poetry in Chile as well as a National Endowment for the Arts Translators Grant in 1988. He lives with his wife and son in Canton, New York, where he teaches at St. Lawrence University.

From the Country of Thunder is the title of his most recent volume of poetry from Unicorn Press, which also has published *Burning the Old Year* and *For the Unborn*, in addition to the following bilingual anthologies he edited and translated: *Poets of Nicaragua: 1918-1979; Poets of Chile: 1965-1985;* and *The Birth of the Sun: Selected Poems of Pablo Antonio Cuadra 1935-1985.* Lumen Books brought out *Culture & Politics in Nicaragua.* His new translation (with Greg Simon) of Federico García Lorca's *Poet in New York* was recently published by Farrar, Straus & Giroux.

Works by Gioconda Belli

Poetry:

Sobre la grama. Managua: INDESA, 1974.
Línea de fuego. Havana: Casa de las Américas, 1978.
Truenos y arco iris. Managua: Nueva Nicaragua, 1982.
Amor insurrecto. Managua: Nueva Nicaragua, 1985.
De la costilla de Eva. Managua: Nueva Nicaragua, 1987.

Prose:

La mujer habitada. Managua: Vanguardia, 1988;
       rpt. Wuppertal, West Germany: Peter Hammer, 1988;
       rpt. Mexico: Diana, 1989.

Related titles available from Curbstone Press

Nicaragua:

HAVE YOU SEEN A RED CURTAIN IN MY WEARY CHAMBER, selected writings by Tomás Borge; edited & trans. by Russell Bartley, Kent Johnson & Sylvia Yoneda. This first U.S. publication of Tomás Borge's poetry, essays and stories offers insight into this man, his work and the Nicaraguan Revolution. $9.95pa.

FLIGHTS OF VICTORY/VUELOS DE VICTORIA, poetry by Ernesto Cardenal edited & trans. by Marc Zimmerman, et al. In this bilingual edition, Cardenal celebrates his country's successful overthrow of the Somoza regime. Deeply religious and revolutionary, Cardenal's poetry is acclaimed throughout the world. $9.95pa.

El Salvador:

ASHES OF IZALCO, a novel by Claribel Alegría and Darwin J. Flakoll, trans. by Darwin J. Flakoll. A love story which unfolds during the bloody events of 1932, when 30,000 Indians and peasants were massacred in Izalco, El Salvador. $17.95cl./$9.95pa.

LUISA IN REALITYLAND, a prose/verse novel by Claribel Alegría; trans. by Darwin J. Flakoll. A retrospect of the real, surreal and magical memories of childhood in El Salvador into which the realities of war gradually intrude. $9.95 pa./$17.95 cl.

ON THE FRONT LINE: Guerrilla Poems of El Salvador, edited & trans. by Claribel Alegría & Darwin J. Flakoll. A bilingual edition. More than poetry of combat, this volume is a record of the struggles, hopes and dreams of a war-torn country. $7.95pa.

MIGUEL MARMOL, by Roque Dalton; trans. by Richard Schaaf. Long considered a classic testimony throughout Latin America, *Miguel Marmol* gives a detailed account of Salvadoran history while telling the interesting and sometimes humorous story of one man's life. $12.95pa./$19.95cl.

Guatemala:

GRANDDAUGHTERS OF CORN: Portraits of Guatemalan Women by Marilyn Anderson & Jonathan Garlock. These photographs of Guatemalan women are accompanied by text that provides background for understanding the cultural as well as political realities in this turbulent country. $19.95pa./$35.00cl.

TESTIMONY: Death of a Guatemalan Village by Victor Montejo; trans. by Victor Perera. *Testimony* gives an eyewitness account by a Mayan school teacher of an army attack on a Guatemalan village and its aftermath, told in a clean and direct prose style. $8.95pa./$16.95cl.

FOR A COMPLETE CATALOG, SEND A REQUEST TO:
Curbstone Press, 321 Jackson St., Willimantic, CT 06226